Helping Your Adopted Child

Understanding Your Child's Unique Identity

Paul David Tripp

New Growth Press
www.newgrowthpress.com

All Scripture quotations, unless otherwise indicated, are taken from the *Holy Bible,* New International Version®, NIV®. Copyright © 1973, 1978, 1984 by International Bible Society. Used by permission of Zondervan. All rights reserved.

New Growth Press, Greensboro, NC 27429
Copyright © 2008 by Christian Counseling & Educational Foundation. All rights reserved. Published 2008

Cover Design: The DesignWorks Group, Nate Salciccioli and Jeff Miller, www.thedesignworksgroup.com

Typesetting: Robin Black, www.blackbirdcreative.biz

ISBN-10: 1-934885-31-2
ISBN-13: 978-1-934885-31-4

Library of Congress Cataloging-in-Publication Data

Tripp, Paul David, 1950-
  Helping your adopted child : understanding your child's unique identity / Paul David Tripp.
     p. cm.
  Includes bibliographical references and index.
  ISBN 978-1-934885-31-4
  1. Adoption—Religious aspects—Christianity. 2. Adopted children. 3. Adoptive parents—Religious life. I. Title.
  HV875.26.T75 2008
  248.8'45—dc22

                                           2008011757

Printed in Canada
10 11 12   5 4 3

I will never forget that day. Our whole family waited in anxious anticipation at the gate reserved for us at the Philadelphia airport. All of a sudden she arrived. The adoption agency representative carried her, face forward, towards us. She was just four months old and had never seen us before, but she smiled from ear to ear. The agency worker placed her in my wife's waiting arms, and we all crumbled into a pool of emotion.

That precious package is now twenty-five years old. The journey of adoption hasn't always been easy, but we are very thankful we made this important choice, and there is absolutely no doubt she is too!

Deciding to be God's agent in the forming of a human soul is one of the most important decisions you will ever make. And it's even more amazing to open your home and heart to a child who is unable to be nurtured by his biological parents. Yet, for all of its beauty, adoption also has significant challenges. Understanding your adopted child from God's perspective will allow you to face those challenges by faith and with hope. Take a moment to read this book. It will help you to think biblically about the choice you made and give you direction on how you can help your adopted child.

In God's Eyes You Are Doing a Good Thing

Defending, loving, nurturing, and providing for a homeless child is very close to the heart of God. It's a concrete expression of the love he has for us and the love he calls us to have for others. God describes himself as a "father to the fatherless" (Psalm 68:5); he tells us to "defend the cause of the fatherless" (Isaiah 1:17); and he uses his people's unwillingness to "plead the case of the fatherless" (Jeremiah 5:28), as evidence of how sinful they had become.

Why is this important to remember? It's

important because the people around you—other members of your family and even your adopted child—will not always recognize the God-honoring beauty of what you are doing. On the hard days when nothing you do seems right and you spend most of your time dealing with conflict and rebellion, you must remind yourself, *What I am doing right now, although hard, is close to God's heart.* And, *What I am doing is exactly what God has called his children to do.*

Adopting Your Child Was God's Plan

In God's world there are no "Plan B" addresses. Just as God planned for your natural children to be born to you, he also planned for this child to be in your home. Long before you made the choice to adopt, long before your child was born, God knew the precious value of his or her life and decided that your home would be the place for this child to receive loving care. The apostle Paul says that God determines the exact place where every person will live (Acts 17:26). Your adopted child is with you because of a wise choice made by a loving God, who cares for you and for the child you have welcomed into your home.

Your Adopted Child Is Unique

God's plan was that children would be raised by their biological parents. But sin entered the world and caused the relational and familial brokenness that sometimes leads to the separation of children from their natural parents. Although you are doing a wonderful thing, you must recognize that children were meant to live with their natural parents. When children are raised by those who aren't their natural parents, there will be struggles and difficulties. Parenting an adopted child is often harder than parenting your natural child. Your adopted child deals with significant personal issues that your natural child never has to deal with.

God planned for parents to pass down physical

and emotional personality traits to their children. Because of the power of family nurture, your adopted child will take on many of your traits, but he will also be unique and different. Your adopted child won't always respond in predictable and comfortable ways. At times he may seem like a stranger in your family, and you will scratch your head and say, "Well, why in the world did he do that?"

Your struggles with your adopted child will not always be the result of your mistakes. Sometimes your struggles will stem from inherent differences in the hardwiring of your child. Those differences will require different parenting strategies from the ones you use with your natural children.

Your Adopted Child Will Struggle with Identity and Place

Every human being asks two questions: "Who am I?" and "Where do I belong?" God's plan was that these profoundly human questions would be answered naturally as children were progressively nurtured in the protective and affirming environment of the day-by-day love of their natural parents.

So when a child is separated from her natural parents, siblings, and culture and has to adjust to new parents, new siblings, and a new culture, she is going to struggle even more with those questions about her identity and where she belongs. What looks like selfishness and rebellion in your adopted child might simply be the way she is coping with her fears and insecurities about her identity and place in the world.

Thankfully, God, in the Bible, has much to say about our identity as his children and our place of belonging in his family. You will have to remind your child again and again that all who believe are adopted into God's family. The apostle John explains this truth by saying, "How great is the love the Father has lavished on us, that we should be called children of God! And that is what we are!" (1 John 3:1).

And you will have to remind your child many

times that she doesn't have to be full of fear about her identity or her place in the world because "you did not receive a spirit that makes you a slave again to fear, but you received the Spirit of sonship. And by him we cry, 'Abba, Father.' The Spirit himself testifies with our spirit that we are God's children. Now if we are children, then we are heirs—heirs of God and co-heirs with Christ, if indeed we share in his sufferings in order that we may also share in his glory" (Romans 8:15–17).

You might wonder why it seems like you have to deal with these issues of identity and belonging with your adopted child over and over again. This is because your adopted child's struggle with his place in life is taking place at the same time as his development. You might deal with a particular struggle when your child is five and think that it's solved. But that same struggle will come up, in a different way, at the age of ten because a ten-year-old is able to feel and understand things that a five-year-old can't. Perhaps that same struggle will rear its head at age twelve and again at age seventeen. It's not that your parenting has been ineffective or that your adopted child has refused to listen; but, with the natural maturation of development, your child has to deal with old issues in new and different ways.

Temptations Your Adopted Child Faces

Your adopted child, like every other child is a sinner. Because she is a sinner, she will be tempted to respond to the natural struggle she has with her place in life sinfully. So she will be tempted to deal with her fears of identity and belonging in a negative way. She might accuse you of playing favorites or of not being fair. She might test your love by challenging your authority. Because she struggles with where she belongs, she might become domineering and controlling. She might try to establish her place by being overly competitive and overly oriented to the boundaries of privacy and possessions.

Because of these temptations, it's very important that you learn how to deal forthrightly with the sinful responses, while demonstrating a loving and patient awareness of the profound struggles underneath. You want your adopted child to be aware that you understand what he is dealing with, but also to know that you will require him to deal with them in the right way.

Remind her daily of the presence and help of the Lord Jesus. God is with her and he promises that he will never leave. God says that "the LORD himself goes before you and will be with you; he will never leave you nor forsake you. Do not be afraid; do not be discouraged" (Deuteronomy 31:8).

And God has promised to give him everything he needs to deal with his life in a way that is right and good. The apostle Peter says, "His divine power has given us everything we need for life and godliness through our knowledge of him who called us by his own glory and goodness. Through these he has given us his very great and precious promises, so that through them you may participate in the divine nature and escape the corruption in the world caused by evil desires" (2 Peter 1:3–4). Remind your child of these promises when you see him struggling.

God Will Help You in Your Weakness

Your Lord is an adoptive Father who welcomes you into his family, even though you did nothing to deserve his love and welcome. He loves you faithfully, even though you mess up again and again. Your adoptive heavenly Father knows exactly what you need as an adoptive parent. He will not turn a deaf ear to your cries. He knows the size and significance of what you have taken on, and he is aware of your limits and weaknesses. The apostle Paul tells us how God helps those who are weak: "But [God] said to me, 'My grace is sufficient for you, for my power is made perfect in weakness.' Therefore I will boast all the more gladly about my weaknesses, so that Christ's power may rest on me" (2 Corinthians 12:9).

God's grace is most powerfully present when you are at your weakest. Adoption will take you beyond the borders of your natural wisdom, love, patience, and strength. But you are not without resources. In your weakness you are the moment-by-moment recipient of the powerful grace of a loving Lord who understands exactly what you are going through.

Practical Strategies for Change

You have learned some things about the particular challenges you face raising your adopted child. How can you apply what you've learned to your adopted child? Below are some practical guidelines to help you. As you read them, remember that each child is unique, so you must rely on God for the spiritual wisdom to know how to apply these strategies to the particular challenges of raising your adopted child.

Be Open about the Adoption

Be open and honest with your child about her adoption. It's very loving to begin early to help your child deal with the unique place God has designed for her in your family. Because you are lovingly open about it, your child will be encouraged to have the same attitude. This will allow you to have productive, daily conversation with your child about how she is dealing with her unique challenges. You will then also have the opportunity to help your child understand some of these challenges and reassure her of your love and God's love.

Aim for Your Child's Heart

Remember that it is not enough to try to regulate your child's behavior, because it is what is in our hearts that controls the things we say and do. Jesus said,

> No good tree bears bad fruit, nor does a bad tree bear good fruit. Each tree is recognized by its own fruit. People do not pick figs from thornbushes, or grapes from briers. The good man brings good things out of the good stored up in his heart, and the evil man brings evil things out of the evil stored

up in his heart. For out of the overflow of his heart his mouth speaks. (Luke 6:43–45)

Since all behavior comes from what is inside us, lasting change in the behavior of your child must start with change in his heart. Setting up systems to control his behavior is good. But if this is your only parenting strategy, it will fail because when he is away from your system he will have nothing internal to control him. When God works real change in the thoughts, attitudes, desires, motives, goals, and values of your child's heart, then his actions and words will change as well.

Questions That Aim at the Heart

You can help your adopted child recognize and admit her heart struggles. All of us can be blind to what's in our hearts (Hebrews 3:12–13). So your adopted child needs your help to identify what heart struggles are beneath her behavioral struggles. I have found a series of questions very helpful in getting children to examine their hearts. Make sure you ask these questions in the order they are in below because each question builds on the previous.

1. *What was going on?* Have your child tell you about the details of the situation.
2. *What where you thinking and feeling as it was happening?* This will help your child look at the thoughts and emotions in her heart.
3. *What did you do in response?* It's important that you ask this third and not second, because your child's behavior comes from her heart.
4. *Why did you do it; what were you seeking to accomplish?* This goes after the purposes, goals, and motives of the heart.
5. *What was the result?* This addresses the consequences of the choices the child made.

Point Your Adopted Child to Jesus

You need to point your adopted child to Jesus Christ every day. The bright and hopeful promise of the life, death, and resurrection of Jesus Christ is a new heart. God promises that he will "give them an undivided heart and put a new spirit in them; [he] will remove from them their heart of stone and give them a heart of flesh" (Ezekiel 11:19).

Jesus has the power to do what we can't: change our hearts. To all who put their faith in him he offers forgiveness and a new, clean heart that wants to love God and others. When he changes our hearts, we are able to do and say things we couldn't have before. The power of Jesus to forgive and change hearts is the hope you need to put before your adopted child again and again as he struggles with his place in life. The rules you give him will instruct him and protect him, but they will never change him from the inside out. Only Jesus can do that!

Go to Jesus Yourself

As you help your child with her struggles, admit your own struggles as well. Parenting a child who is unhappy, challenging, or rebellious is hard. It takes unusual love, grace, patience, and perseverance. Daily run to your Lord and confess your struggles to him. Quietly ask people who know and love you to pray for you. Be willing to be held accountable. And resist the temptation to be pulled into a personal war with someone you have chosen to love. When you don't deal with your own heart issues, the following things will happen:

- You will personalize what is not personal. You will see your child's struggles as all about you, instead of about your child and her relationship with God.
- Because you have done this, you will turn a moment of ministry into a moment of anger.
- Because you are now angry, you will be adversarial in your response.
- As a result, you will settle for quick lectures and punishments that don't really address

your child's heart or the deeper issues behind her struggles.

But as you go to Jesus with your own struggles and ask him to change your own heart and fill you with his Spirit, you will be able to respond constructively and kindly to your child's challenging behavior.

Teach Your Child About Identity in Christ

Because your adopted child will struggle with issues of identity, he will be tempted to look for identity in all the wrong things. He will look for identity in *other people* and be hurt and disappointed again and again. He will look for identity in *achievement* and become driven and competitive. He will look for identity in *material things* and become selfish, possessive, and materialistic. He will look for identity in *power and position* and become dominant and controlling. All of these ways of securing identity will not satisfy him—they will only enslave him.

To counter these tendencies you must constantly work to root your adopted child's identity in Christ. When your child begins to grasp the truth that, although he can't earn God's love, he has been fully, deeply, and eternally accepted in Christ, he will be able to be at peace with who he is and where God has placed him. Then, no matter what struggles of acceptance and belonging he faces, he will have the comfort of knowing he is fully accepted by the Ruler of the universe, and no person or circumstance will be able to separate him from God's love (Romans 8:31–39).

You also, as the parent of an adopted child, have to know and rely on the love God has for you (1 John 4:16). Only as you do so will you be able to put these principles into practice and daily treat your adopted child with the same patience and kindness that your heavenly Father has for you.

If you were encouraged by reading this booklet, perhaps you or someone you know would also be blessed from these booklets:

Angry Children: Understanding and Helping Your Child Regain Control, by Michael R. Emlet, M.Div., M.D.

Breaking Pornography Addiction: Strategies for Lasting Change by David Powlison, M.Div., Ph.D.

Controlling Anger: Responding Constructively When Life Goes Wrong by David Powlison, M.Div., Ph.D.

Divorce Recovery: Growing and Healing God's Way by Winston T. Smith, M.Div.

Eating Disorders: The Quest for Thinness by Edward T. Welch, M.Div., Ph.D.

Facing Death with Hope: Living for What Lasts by David Powlison, M.Div., Ph.D.

Family Feuds: How to Respond by Timothy S. Lane, M.Div., D.Min.

Freedom from Addiction: Turning from Your Addictive Behavior by Edward T. Welch, M.Div., Ph.D.

Freedom from Guilt: Finding Release from Your Burdens by Timothy S. Lane, M.Div., D.Min.

Healing after Abortion: God's Mercy Is for You by David Powlison, M.Div., Ph.D.

Help for Stepfamilies: Avoiding the Pitfalls and Learning to Love by Winston T. Smith, M.Div.

Help for the Caregiver: Facing the Challenges with Understanding and Strength by Michael R. Emlet, M.Div., M.D.

Help! My Spouse Committed Adultery: First Steps for Dealing with Betrayal by Winston T. Smith, M.Div.

Hope for the Depressed: Understanding Depression and Steps to Change by Edward T. Welch, M.Div., Ph.D.

How Do I Stop Losing It with My Kids? Getting to the Heart of Your Discipline Problems by William P. Smith, M.Div., Ph.D.

How to Love Difficult People: Receiving and Sharing God's Mercy by William P. Smith, M.Div., Ph.D.

Living with an Angry Spouse: Help for Victims of Abuse by Edward T. Welch, M.Div., Ph.D.

Overcoming Anxiety: Relief for Worried People by David Powlison, M.Div., Ph.D.

Peer Pressure: Recognizing the Warning Signs and Giving New Direction by Paul David Tripp, M.Div., D.Min.

Recovering from Child Abuse: Healing and Hope for Victims by David Powlison, M.Div., Ph.D.

Renewing Marital Intimacy: Closing the Gap Between You and Your Spouse by David Powlison, M.Div., Ph.D.

Should We Get Married? How to Evaluate Your Relationship by William P. Smith, M.Div., Ph.D.

Single Parents: Daily Grace for the Hardest Job, by Robert D. Jones, M.Div., D.Min.

When Bad Things Happen: Thoughtful Answers to Hard Questions by William P. Smith, M.Div., Ph.D.

When Marriage Disappoints: Hope and Help by Paul David Tripp, M.Div., D.Min.

Who Does the Dishes? Decision Making in Marriage by Winston T. Smith, M.Div.

To learn more about CCEF visit our website at www.ccef.org.